Wheels, Wings, and Water
ABC

Lola M. Schaefer

Heinemann Library
Chicago, Illinois

© 2003 Heinemann Library
a division of Reed Elsevier Inc.
Chicago, Illinois

Customer Service 888-454-2279
Visit our website at www.heinemannlibrary.com

Designed by Heinemann Library; Page layout by Que-Net Media
Printed and bound in the United States by Lake Book Manufacturing, Inc.
Photo research by Amor Montes De Oca

07 06 05 04 03
10 9 8 7 6 5 4 3 2 1

Library of Congress Cataloging-in-Publication Data
Schaefer, Lola M., 1950-
   Wheels, wings, and water ABC / Lola Schaefer.
      p. cm. — (Wheels, wings, and water)
Includes index.
Summary: Photographs and simple text depict various forms of transportation and related concepts, from airplanes to rockets that "zoom" into space.
   ISBN 1-4034-0887-4 (HC), 1-4034-3625-8 (Pbk.)
   1. Motor vehicles—Juvenile literature. 2. Alphabet books. [1. Motor vehicles. 2. Transportation. 3. Alphabet.] I. Title.
II. Series.
   TL147 .S373 2003
   629.04'6—dc21

2002014728

Acknowledgments
The author and publishers are grateful to the following for permission to reproduce copyright material:
pp. 3, 10 Jeffrey Howe/Visuals Unlimited; p. 4 John Welzenbach/Corbis; p. 5 James A. Sugar/Corbis; p. 6 Jane Faircloth/Transparencies, Inc.; p. 7 Jeff Greenberg/Visuals Unlimited; p. 8 Gary J. Benson; p. 9 AL, Linda Bristor/Visuals Unlimited; p. 11 Mark E. Gibson/Visuals Unlimited; p. 12 NASA/Corbis; p. 13 Larry Williams/Corbis; p. 14 Corbis; pp. 15, 21 Amor Montes De Oca; p. 16 Richard Hamilton Smith/Corbis; p. 17 Jeff Greenberg/TRIP; p. 18 Tiziana and Gianni Baldizzone/Corbis; p. 19L Duomo/Corbis; p. 19R Jim McDonald/Corbis; p. 20 Dick Reed/Corbis; p. 22 Science VU/NASA/JPL/Visuals Unlimited; p. 23 row 1 (L-R) NASA/Corbis, Doug Wilson/Corbis, Science VU/NASA/JPL/Visuals Unlimited; row 2 (L-R) Richard Hamilton Smith/Corbis, Photodisc, Jonathan Blair/Corbis, Jim McDonald/Corbis; row 3 (L-R) Jane Faircloth/Transparencies, Inc., PictureNet/Corbis, Jeff Greenberg/TRIP, Dick Reed/Corbis; row 4 (L-R) Jeff Greenberg/Visuals Unlimited, Kent Foster/Visuals Unlimited, Tiziana and Gianni Baldizzone/Corbis, Amor Montes De Oca; back cover (L-R) James A. Sugar/Corbis, Jane Faircloth/Transparencies, Inc.

Cover photographs by George D. Lepp/Corbis, Dennis Marsico/Corbis, James A. Sugar/Corbis

Every effort has been made to contact copyright holders of any material reproduced in this book. Any omissions will be rectified in subsequent printings if notice is given to the publisher.

Special thanks to our advisory panel for their help in the preparation of this book:
Alice Bethke, Library Consultant
Palo Alto, CA

Eileen Day, Preschool Teacher
Chicago, IL

Kathleen Gilbert,
Second Grade Teacher
Round Rock, TX

Sandra Gilbert,
Library Media Specialist
Fiest Elementary School
Houston, TX

Jan Gobeille,
Kindergarten Teacher
Garfield Elementary
Oakland, CA

Angela Leeper,
Educational Consultant
North Carolina Department
of Public Instruction
Wake Forest, NC

Some words are shown in bold, **like this.**
You can find them in the picture glossary on page 23.

A a Airplane

wing

tail

N4630N

An airplane can fly through the air.

Airplanes have wings and a tail.

Bb Bicycle

Bicycles have two wheels.

Many children ride bicycles to school.

C c   Canoe

paddle

Canoes are long, thin boats.

People use paddles to push canoes.

D d   Dirt Bike

People call BMX bicycles dirt bikes.

Dirt bikes race on **dirt tracks.**

E e   Engine

hood

Engines help cars move.

Most car engines are under the hood.

F f Fire Trucks

Fire trucks carry firefighters and their tools.

G g   Gas Tank

gas tank

Gas tanks hold gasoline.

Gasoline makes motorcycles go.

H h   Helicopter

Helicopters can fly up, down, or sideways.

They can even fly in one place.

I i Inner Tube

Some boats pull **inner tubes** through the water.

People ride on inner tubes for fun.

Jj Jetpack

jetpack

Jetpacks help **astronauts** move through space.

Astronauts wear jetpacks on their backs.

Kayak

paddle

Kayaks are boats that can go on rivers and lakes.

People use paddles to make kayaks move.

Ll Locomotive

Locomotives push or pull the cars of a train.

M m   Motorcycle

trailer

Some motorcycles are very large.

This touring motorcycle has a trailer.

N n   Nose
O o   Oval

nose

The front of a **blimp** is called the nose.

Blimps are shaped like **ovals.**

P p   Passengers
Q q   Quarterdeck

Passengers are on this ship.

Sometimes they look at the sea from the **quarterdeck**.

R r Raft
S s Steer

Most **rafts** are flat boats made of wood.

People steer rafts with poles.

T t Tricycle
U u Unicycle

unicycle

Tricycles have three wheels.

Unicycles have one wheel.

V v Van
W w Windshield

windshield

Vans are large cars that can carry many people.

Windshields keep **passengers** safe from rain, snow, and wind.

Xx Extra Hoses
Yy Gated-Y

Sometimes firefighters need extra hoses.

They use a **gated**-Y to put two hoses together.

Z z   Zoom!

This **rocket** zooms into space.

Picture Glossary

astronaut
page 12

gas tank
page 9

kayak
page 13

quarterdeck
page 17

blimp
page 16

gated-Y
page 21

locomotive
page 14

raft
page 18

dirt track
page 6

inner tube
page 11

oval
page 16

rocket
page 22

engine
page 7

jetpack
page 12

passengers
pages 17, 20

unicycle
page 19

Note to Parents and Teachers

Using this book, children can practice alphabetic skills while learning interesting facts about various modes of transportation. Together, read *Wheels, Wings, and Water ABC*. Say the names of the letters aloud, then say the target word, exaggerating the beginning of the word. For example, "/r/: Rrrr-aft." Can the child think of any other words that begin with the /r/ sound? (Although the letter x is not at the beginning of the word "extra," the /ks/ sound of the letter x is still prominent.) Try to sing the "ABC Song," substituting the *Wheels, Wings, and Water* alphabet words for the letters a, b, c, and so on.

Index